SOLDIER ON

SOLDIER ON

poems by GALE MARIE THOMPSON

NORTH ADAMS, MASSACHUSETTS

Soldier On

Copyright © 2015 Gale Marie Thompson. All rights reserved.

Library of Congress Cataloging-in-Publication Data
Thompson, Gale Marie, 1986–
[Poems. Selections]
Soldier on : poems / by Gale Marie Thompson.
    pages cm
 Summary: "The light of the kitchen is a starting and ending point when exploring
remembered spaces, which take on new facets and textures in the mind's endless
cross-indexing" -- Provided by publisher.
 ISBN 978-1-936797-55-4 (pbk. : alk. paper)
 I. Title.
 PS3620.H664A6 2015
 811'.6--dc23
                        2014044193

First paperback edition: January 2015.

Tupelo Press
P.O. Box 1767, North Adams, Massachusetts 01247
Telephone: (413) 664–9611 / editor@tupelopress.org / www.tupelopress.org

Tupelo Press is an award-winning independent literary press that publishes fine
fiction, nonfiction, and poetry in books that are a joy to hold as well as read.
Tupelo Press is a registered 501(c)(3) nonprofit organization, and we rely on
public support to carry out our mission of publishing extraordinary work that may
be outside the realm of the large commercial publishers. Financial donations are
welcome and are tax deductible.

A certain minor light may still

Lean incandescent

Out of kitchen table or chair

— *Sylvia Plath*

(light on the kitchen table early morning, etc.)

— *Joseph Cornell*

CONTENTS

SOLDIER ON

CILANTRO BLUE

Something has been gnawing
at my screen all weekend.
·The dress I put on weighs nothing,
is pinned in every place possible.
You can see it wishing us
a public good morning.
This is the kitchen in clean makeup.
This is the sound of a building when it breathes.
The glow of flour, blown sugar in cricket lace.
Dear Retrospect, pick my brain.
We will say anything. You say.
Anything is a harbor. Anything is singing.
Stay close. The drum in me starts,
says, *welcome, orbit.*
Welcome Horoscope,
Welcome Kissing Gate.
Push on my kidneys, bury my Atlantic.
I will have my hands in this deluge.
Come be swept up & sieved
& enter & enter & enter.

YES, BUT MORE ANIMALS

I am here dreaming of the Okavango, of lean times.
I keep thinking of my mouth without your mouth,
lobe-finned fishes, jackrabbits in their burrows.
There's a true science to how I dress.
When I walk I like to watch the great rumble
of my thighs find the light.
I want to hold sand against my chest but think twice.
Nothing is real to me unless it's right in front of me.
Is this enough bravado for you?
I want to give you the shape of a home,
but only if it's the right one.
I want you to cry when I tell you the bad news,
like *the breeze takes away every warm thing,* and
I did the best I could with all the decades.

GOD BLESS SVALBARD

When I shower next to Svalbard
I put my hands to my chest.
A movement similar to opening up the Andes
and finding beautiful crickets inside.
I float up and down.
I flash in and out of sight.
I have a strong impulse to be
the perfect listener in another room.
The meaning of Sunday
gets smaller and smaller.
When you are sleeping I am a real thief.
I am not here for the season.
I steal your little goose egg
and pollute just about everything.
I take off my clothes
and eat a late lunch with you
but you are sorry for Svalbard,
the twelve men burning in Spain.

FOREST/CITY POEM

These are our gifts: we are young and healthy and go to
the convenience store, our heavenly bodies full of
cement. We being blackened, and entirely not dead. I
tell you I love you, I love you so much. I tell you the
boreal forest puts me to sleep. I want to think that the
Earth will always be warm, but that will take some time
to believe in.

CAVE/CITY POEM

Our door is a beautiful door. When I open it I will be a
new religion. I will drink the last of the wine and become
so alive with the smell of caraway and sausage. I will heat
the ovens with my hands. I will bring you a jar of fen-
nel seeds soaked in milk. Inside these burnished walls,
astonishment. In this little box we marry for ages.

OCEAN/CITY POEM

You are in another house. A house of salt water, of rust, an undertaking. Wood stars on the ceiling. I will be back soon with a new kind of radio, my voice in the car. I will bring you a new room filled with wine. Somehow we will get the baby home. Having been here for so long, we have gotten used to everything. We are ready to sell, ready to move on.

SUSPENDED ON A RIGID STRING

Today it feels like I'm talking to you
through a tundra
Possible to say it was the snowbirds
Possible to be underfoot
I am the wind barreling through dark wool
Kind and blindsided and in a blue sweater always
You are number one spirit guide
A memorandum for a given name
My hands out of order
All swollen and folded into drawers
Instead of saying gingham I should have said
I am washing my hands
I should have gone barefoot
But my friends wanted me to call you
Because the dark swells like sabayon
And we are the grim orange

THE MOST BEAUTIFUL BIBLES

The kitchens are beautiful but migrating,
and there's shoeshine all over the floor.
It's shipwrecked. It's heliocentric.
I love your head-butt maneuver.
Your thundering goatherds.
Something keeps coming, so let's
put some joy into it.
We are in the future perfect
and we are wearing hats.
I have this nightlight. It's the only
medium we're stepping on.
It's not as settled as it should be, is it?
Let's be a facsimile of sloughing
skin cells. Let's clear out the palimpsest.
Here's me nodding my head.
Here's the jubilee year.
Someone is selling us dozens
of Egyptian apartments.
We keep on eating and receiving
bad news in the mail. We are inexhaustible.
We can do shots off my dent.
We are putting something together
and you are coming round.
Good thing you're not red.
Good thing you like weather.
Sometimes bad children will have moon-faces.

Sometimes you don't want to take off your shoes.

Here, let me cover you with sapphires.

Let me see your staircase puddle.

It's not as if we can't stand for hours

bent this way.

POEM TO JOHN WAYNE

The bunkers are loud how loud
can it be at the end of the world
where there are twelve of you
and you are green and full of women
and everyone waits their turn
thumbs heavy on the t-shirts

green beret I want you
to see Thursday my favorite
green beret heap of mechanic
there are days when you are bursting
in the middle of a highway

since March, nonstop

my eyes are burning
if I knew what a bunker was
I could help you out

*

In the morning by the blackberries
there are rollers in my hair
warm pimientos handed to me
the nickname Cactus and then
the worry of
being remembered

I want green
I want getting old
to prepare me
for getting old
or else how
can I remember
the memory
of saying
good night

*

Say I am the one who slept
beside a jar of crickets
I have become
land-loving and a pilgrim
kept always barefoot
watching folks kiss on TV

what's all this ballyhoo, anyway?
will you marry it?

*

Everyone can watch each other
grow old by the seastacks
there is an islet baking
in the Carolina room

and from where you are
the sun is just
and God is
unjust

how can you hear
how much can you hear
after the water polo

*

Watch your stomach grow
my favorite
little big man I have come
from Waukesha
to see you lilt

It's like
I haven't shown you
how quiet I can be
back in the twin's bedroom

where the crickets got out
and we lost Davy Crockett
I lost the stole
the dress from Hawaii
the duvet covers
I want to keep the light on
I want davy crockett davy crockett
davy crockett if we can get
to the airport we can stop this
but that's not
for today

IF ALKALINE, IF EXTINCTION

Your problems are a body of water
and when I have these things to tell you
it means that mostly I enjoy the way you say posies.
I have forty salt licks and glands for days.
We can both be a little reborn, if you'd like.
I want nothing more than to entertain you.
Give you a legend.
Such as, there are several ways to expand
but perhaps this is not the best one.
We never knew other quiet things.
We shared an entire police station.
We shared a passion for beach hats.
Now this month's divots are puddling on the floor
with this month's missing gemstone.
I am thinking that time
is something we move through.
I am missing so many bees these days.
Inside drawers, a carafe of whipping cream.
Crack a rib, and birds fly out of a spoon.

FULL AND FALL

Being warm, it rains
The mysterious farm

Thaws, startling hands
Somewhere sun

Becoming a path
Out onto the sidewalk

Very welcome
This renewal

I need reminding of cars
Of fruit, half-peeled

To get it down
Skin and skimming

Can any part be measured
Can I measure this

You sleeping under me
One more time

Together in the kitchen
Blue in the cafeteria

Tomorrow being morning
Or someplace near

MOBILES

Unbelievable
to look at my face
young bones in the house
I grew sick in

Until now I have been waiting
to see the most evidence

What did not exist
in the prior week

*

Entirely apology
there was exactly this:

canning the figs before they died
cooking onions until creamy
and translucent
opalescent

I'm afraid my shatter
is beginning to define me

*

If I eat at the theater
and sing that I love you rough
it is not the same love all the time

Happy maintenances
people as audience noise

A nice little space
where you can do
what you should do

The weather started it
please read this

*

He is underground
and she wants to show him the baby

one morning
tiny and silver

Nothing to say except
Yes, there may be

no particular party
in the sky

*

Wherever the end may be
if my eyesight gets better
I can see further and further out

I can warm my face
with palms still blazing
This is not love

I do not love this

*

Here is the water
my soggy fingers
When I wake up I won't be dead

There is a moth outside my door

I leave
it is a steeplechase.

DUPLEX

At first everything was going beautifully,
undressing, treading water.
Now I drink my body out in the kitchen.
I am thinking of arranging
the cat's playthings to stop the flooding.
It's easy to understand this quest for new pasture.
A long migration through ceramic French doors.

If you come over today I will clean the fish for you.
I have these gingersnaps and a jar of watermelon.
Come, guess which state I'm from,
guess which morning I picked these turnips for you.
Give me a laugh, and I will pick you up.
It's always warmest when a baby's around.

Today someone broke the sugar bowl.
Someone brought the decanter. If we are lucky
it will still smell of peaches and zinfandel,
all quite beautiful and buzzing.
If we are lucky we can see the turnip fields from here,
glowing and torpedoed from the rain.

YELLOW FROSTED CAKE

Whitewash makes me hungry.

Astronomy does too.

We are muscle flowers in the shape of marzipan.

We are a trick. We paint comet after comet

onto the faces of cakes,

wipe the nebulae off of our fingers,

call it *assemblage*.

It is too early for fondant.

Wherever we are it is soggy.

Wherever I am there are mouthfuls.

Last night I dreamed I made you soup

in a steel kitchen.

I sat on your floor and glowed.

There is too much in our gold, planetary bodies.

There's no keeping it down.

Today there are instincts ingrained in my knuckles.

There are my knuckles, pummeled white.

There are these two legs crowing

under these two socks.

HINGE
for Joseph Cornell

Just within reach of the copper alcove,

now on a bicycle you find you can arrange

and rearrange obsessions,

find the wheatglass and starlings, the milky white

before it fades.

Give me serpentine dance.

Give me prehensile.

Take the color of my follicles as a warning.

It was almost as if, or did you say,

I am going to lose this word? I find myself charged

in the warmth of two people eating together.

I flake everything with red pepper.

My scarf smells like a city.

Make it scientific. Make it not about consumption.

Be ready to show the face flown,

the system of exchange.

A bell blanches in the air.

You catch a darling note.

EARLY LETTERS, UNDATED

What a future
Legs pinned on the internet

Little blue flower of
It is just not the time

Families being only pieces
Of everything

Am I losing my sense
Of magic

Where is that hot day
The boy on his bicycle

Falling into the canal
So much for this

Lightheartedness
These days

On the windowpanes
Blackout papers

Cold birds at breakfast time
I am thinking of nothing else

What doesn't alter
Bodies pinned and finished

As tar paper
It's all about to

Look up
From here

PULSAR

And so said, and so you said
I want to go
with you, without you.
I only wanted for to see
the spectral light.
So lucked out,
so catching,
so dwelled.

*

When one of us goes missing
so missiles,
so signals out
into the arena.
And then what us,
only one us,
what if it is the wrong us.

*

Instead of radio signals
we send cablegrams
that say
such physical ailment,
such taking care of children
on top of all that
so temporary,
so falsehood,
so sweetened heirloom.

*

So we inhabit one station.
Click closed,
so one wall says
to the other
so grid,
so hereafter.
We open one inch
so becoming reunited,
so chrome
so this arrow, frozen.

*

So lost, we sleep.

So the house is clean.

So what we choose

is what is chosen

always

and so it is

until we, deafened,

sleep.

ONE OF NATURE'S MASTERPIECES

There is a crowd of parents
around me tonight.
The fact that we are perishing
is the easiest to understand.
I didn't know anything before my brain existed
and I'm afraid I won't know anything after.
I need to be occupied with something
other than the kitchen radio,
that growing feeling stuck to my ribs.
I want to dance my little heart out
until I shimmer off the walls.
I want the jubilant dance, that early thing.
I want the sound we make
when we are naked and dancing
and connected with everyone,
the fur and the dancing.
Being reborn is like stumbling
against the water, full as a bell.
My family is made of milk
and a general feeling in the vertebrae.
There is smoke on my sweater.
My sweater is my family.

POEM TO JOHN DENVER

It is me, sinking at the bottom of the pool.

It looks like hopeful, almost.

Something not an appetite.

When I say I am thinking of self-portraiture

I am really thinking *loveseat*

over and over.

This town is making me itch,

and I am late in all the shipbuilding.

Instead I begin to tell jokes

in the backyard,

into the compost bin.

Heavy on the turnips.

Have you already forgotten about turnips?

Once, I almost touched your house.

I almost made a little noise,

persimmon in hand, flat like a tomato.

Existence is having a form.

No more will I race uphill

thinking *delicacy, restlessness.*

This mountain is famous

because, because.

EARTH IN SPACE

If there is no sun
and won't be for a while,
I just can't see making it any further.
I keep drifting away in small boats
being a trumpeter, being shapes.
Red and blue are on either side of me,
making impressions of dinosaurs
on plaster of Paris.
I will be broadcast forever. I am so big.
I've got these bones in a rolling boil,
and I have to say
that the human capacity
for darkness baffles me.
Where are there movements?
Where is summer
and the yellow bird?
Please keep me in. Believe me,
I used to be little.
I used to be even littler
and half-looked at the catfish
breathing on the water.
They glow,
they just glow.

EARTH MOVEMENTS

It is right now a jubilee year
and my back is shining
and I have been tromping
on so many orbits
waiting for something to happen
that I have since
become immovable.
I don't think I've mentioned how
my shoulders keep dazzling
and where there are lines
there are times
and places
that I am to meet everyone.
It's all over out there, I've heard.
I mean, I am finding it hard
to fan out the weather balloons,
what with all this cross-draft.
The swimming pools lean
far enough away
to see the earth bow out.
The ellipses have been quiet
for a while now.
It would be impossible to
talk on the phone after this.

MAPPING THE WORLD

Out here I am cross-legged and humming,
and as much as I hate to say it,
the sky is orange twice over.
There is no end
to the gore of mapmaking.
The lights are covered with pudding.
I have become too involved
with the Pacific,
slept on their carpets,
with their passengers.
I wear too much. Inside I am shoeshine,
all earthbound and entertaining.
In the beginning there was a skyline
that I could wriggle through, glistening.
Now the shape of things
has me glassy-eyed.
I've got it this time, almost entirely.
I want to take this to the skyscrapers.
I want to overflow the pages with land.

DEEPAK CHOPRA

Deepak Chopra is round as a sleeping bear and just warm enough. He says that God sings like a tenor and I ask him if he's mistaking God for Pavarotti and he says nothing after that. His hands are full of sponge cake.

Because I can't hear anything I say *Deepak Chopra Deepak Chopra* over and over in my head and I listen, because I always pay the most attention to spiritualists. Deepak Chopra carries two men in his hands the way I want to carry two men, like they are aphorisms. I am hiding from Deepak Chopra behind a cup of tea because he is all about less & less and I'm not at all about that, but he's invented intelligent design so there's nothing more I can do.

Deepak Chopra believes me all the time. Deepak Chopra spells the words *Deepak Chopra* into scattered Scrabble letters, and melts crayons over them. Deepak Chopra believes in aeronautics, and wants more than anything to know why a wing changes shape on takeoff and landing. When I consider orbiting, Deepak Chopra cools my vertebrae. Deepak Chopra is involved with the theory of hypersonic flow, and plans to insert his body into a bottle rocket. To be lifelike. To sing like gas turbine.

AMERICAN BONES, DEAR FRIEND

Here especially, I'd like to see someone
in the front seat of my car, being an angel
or something much more edible.
We're just looking at finger potatoes here.
I'd like to know how to walk and see
at the same time. I'd like to know the cityscape.
Anything is liturgical. Anything is healing wounds
and peat moss, a glass dashboard with white hands inside.
How I want to make out is how I want to see
and be in cahoots with. It's almost as if
my friends are real, have jokes, quit smoking,
hide themselves in drawers for aunts
and other loved ones to find them
wrapped in celebrations and tablebedding.
Or perhaps we're at the point
where hipbones fight holy wars,
and if anyone could get on the air
they would ask about my carbon ring,
my family full of sleeper cells.
All I know is I would shave my entire body to be soft.
I would make the same film over and over again.

QUESTIONS OF COMETS

Space is one giant coin pocket. You may think it looks empty but nothing could be further from the truth. Sometimes space is so delicate and full that decades crawl into water towers and the place we've kept our bed is very much defunct. I can be sure that more delicious things will happen this fiscal year. The comets will brim with change. We will give birth to a baby with two names and two silver spoons and encouraging eyes. We will buy a pasta machine and fill ourselves to the brim. It is natural to want to be a doting parent, to want everything undressed and painted white. It is like our secret name for rhododendron when I say: I am who's got your back when your back is doeskin.

*

What have we got to show for our bodies? What have we to look forward to? Outside, the lantanas share in our act of shimmering. My hands make the shape of a waterfall. I want to buy a welcome mat with *Shalom* on it. I want ten-pound bags of russet potatoes; one after another, after another. I want eggs over easy at the table on the porch.

*

Being unkempt is feeling an open window day and celebrating it. It is hiding in bedrooms to give everyone a break. In the morning we watch the tile pushing beneath our hands. There is nothing less than the sun and the pushing, and we are in hardly any clothing and it is time for the waterfall.

SIGOURNEY WEAVER

Sometimes things get so dark that I forget about brothers.
I forget the burst of white in the kitchen
when cakes become electricity.
I forget about the tundra, and the great snowy plains.
Inside my body are hundreds of bright bulbs
spinning and spinning.
My backyard is a web of camellias.
I have so much optimism
that when I look around me I squint.
All I want is for someone to let me love them, all of them.
I'd always trust them until they broke my heart.
They say snow monkeys have the greatest sense of love.
Last night I had a dream that my mother was Sigourney Weaver.
She stitched me up after my body and everything else split open.
She could smell the top of my head and know I was hers.
We were sitting there on the couch
and outside the moon rose over and over again.

CONTAINERS

I have decided to fold myself into the cupboards, too hefty and white to crouch forward so. I think this is how the birds in your painting feel. I don't think to tell you about this dreary business, how I find it hard to digest. How I go out into the kitchen at night to fill my mouth with peppers. Someone's hands are over you, and your only response is to grow even longer. This is the one thing I can tell you about free will. We pray over tomatillos in the kitchen garden. They glow purple for us in the moonlight, full as balloons.

*   *   *

If you could be any bear, you would be a black bear. You would know absolutely nothing and treat everyone as they would want to be treated. Everything you say sounds amazing. So far I can fill bowlfuls of you. I suspect you will always be in a bathtub. I have thought of all the compost you would create just lying there, book in hand. The sodden pages. You are a child's taste of basil. I look at you and your neck is ecstatic. I can stay awake all night if you need me to, and I can drive even farther.

HOUDINI POEM

This lean house
your other door

What glove
with dust and snow

Whose bed
are you sleeping in
being everywhere

and also here

I missed the fashion
You have your best

and can be beheld
and also expanded

A glass fills with water
and breaks

and when the snow comes
what remains

is the sky
glowing and filled
with black spots

Who are you
when you are absent
from me

PANELS

Overheard, let this exist
and fix or be fixed
as we cannot be in water
or in these cold clouds

Being no longer the smallest creature
a throwing open of the door

I say properly the dawn
has no real warmth

*

You find snow on the balcony

an unfoldment
giving, give out

I will come home on two planes
when I leave I leave the tea bitter

*

I am dividing this house
or the train we sat in
as in

here I am blocking the sun
with my ceramic body

A backward television glow
in the main room

on the counter

*

I want to eat citrus with you
in a warm field

Do not surprise me
with the moment
as I am not prepared for it

*

This has been and will be here
is coterminous
is the naming of what you are

that pushes against it

I can see you
behind the house
flushing in the garden

making the leaves black
with your fire

DUPUYTREN'S CONTRACTURE

Genetic disease is in our teeth.
It sparkles in ribbons and knocks us blindly over.
It begins a new day for the carriage drivers.
They hand us baby girls to apologize to, and we do.
They drive around and around in circles,
sifting the early morning into animal powder.
They are the whitest.
Day after day absorbs from us. Soon we'll see it all
and disappear. And there is no word for it.
The fizzling afterlife. Don't tell anyone,
but the devil dreams in parallel lines.
Another baby with my skin lives in the house.
I keep keeping quiet so you'd think my heart was tough.
Let's talk about the open handfuls of furniture.
Let's dust for photons and send them flying.
This is the last time someone will say our names.

GLASS EYE POEM

Bones are bones
and eyes are replaceable

The sea otters have hands for you
you for the night awake

*

The unbelievably sheer chance
a long wash missed out on

when I heard you sing
on the radio

An uphill glowing Amazon

*

Mostly if not all muscle
you said *my teeth are banded*
so my jaw always aches

*

You knitted the smallest
yarn babies
in a seahorse pouch
matted with shampoo

Natural battle feelings
sconces on hedges
your head one-third shaved

cheekbones
a piggy-bank

It needs to be the most beautiful
eye in the world
to match you

*

At the airport
your mouth is Jupiter

I mail a package of bird seed and amaranth
They would hope inside of you

I am building your room
your stomach
with nothing but rubber bands
Them as we are

Half-lit in the desert,
see: pale morning bones

*

Vowels mark cold spots
in the sky

I want to build you
something archaic

so that in profile it blooms.

COME TO THE KITCHEN, KELSEY

I will make you something clean.
I will swallow now
the city. You are not lost, you are here
in the hallway.
Here it is enough.

Vapor croons fivefold. Even the jars
are rising, the room unspooled
and glazed.
What is a Holy Year?
What is our whitefish terror?
What is Texas?

I have sewn maps onto the bathroom tile.
I have changed my bed-sheets.
I like mannerisms. I like all of this.
If you leave this house
we will carry the dishes with us.
We will roll them to the park with us
and kiss the bulldogs.

I can hold your mouth open
she said

I am still alive
she said

hand me the wooden spoon

THE TODAY SHOW

This morning they are cutting a woman in half.
Her insides ring like a balloon and I pull away from the set.
Outside our door, moths purr
and I am holding an invisible sun to surprise you.
I'd like this to be true science.
I'd like my flammable arms to glow as I type to you
This is the forest? And then you would reply
Oh no, this is the ocean.
Where we live it will be both.

God rearranges things in all the right seasons.
Before this morning everything was new.
The boy who threw the touchdown was alive
and my apron still tugged at my neck.
On this side of the world there are mothers
and great mountains.
Arms overflowing with bunting.
This is the day of the Everglades,
of the best news in the world.

BEWITCHED

Everything is starting to grow on me.

Scottsdale, Arizona, for one. Andrew Jackson,

the new Darren in *Bewitched*.

Now in the gymnasium I lose my head.

A glow rises on my pale stomach that lasts and lasts.

It's getting too magnetic, and I'm not primed nor pink enough.

I may as well take off all my clothes and sit in a stable

full of clean, sparkling water.

When I watch infomercials into the night

the TV makes me think of country.

Bombs make it all the way to my bed.

Today they rescued baby barn owls that look like ghouls.

They are so white.

I want their heads to stop swaying like they have no bones.

I want flowers to take up to Judge Lord.

I want daughters to keep loving their mothers.

There is nothing left but mothers and fossils.

COWARD ORDER

What to find
where does one find it
in motion

a pile of sweaters
on the bed, meaning
not a body has been here
in weeks.

Children are time passing.
You could listen
or not.

I wasn't drunk,
I only refused your offer politely.
Then I jumped into the pool
with my clothes on.

I only wanted to be alive
when the animals are alive.

*

Remember me
and my old face,
standing, a candle
to your other weather.

Eventually matted
becoming unmatted,
a house
with no door,

a burst of crossing
on the portico steps,
white sails
when I am driving home
in the dark
by the farmhouses.

＊

Am I good
because of this virus?
Is what is holding me
to the earth
going to fling me away?

Everything that comes
in front of me
will not get warm
or keep warm.

*

I may not go
to the door.
I may come back to it
five years from now.

This, being absorbed.

This is my shining hour.

UPLOCK

Everyone else we know has a livelihood.

Everyone else has prepared for the dry season.

Never have we seen so many deadbolts.

I am shooting something here,

something of ours with a name.

You look like you, only thirty years older.

I look like a pavilion.

A veranda spotted on the way home.

I am too superstitious.

I yawn too much for your liking,

and unplug planets in my sleep.

My gardenias keep blooming and blooming.

When you weren't looking,

I pocketed you.

You miss someone else

like I miss an orbiting body.

I am goodbye in root vegetables.

I am uneaten. I will always be uneaten.

So let's go ahead and get married,

if only for the mortgage.

Our loan will be in baby food.

We can go to the show in our Sunday best,

right before the Matinee prices end

and hand each other daffodils in the dark.

SOLDIER ON

I am becoming more and more deadbeat
with this star on my stomach.
Put your hand on my spotlight.
Together we can paint
eggshells like blankets,
we can lick sandpaper
for its red flavor.

This is not a tapestry
but something else
in our mouths:
a pendulum, a window.

In this house there is a sink.

In this house there is another house.

A house of hobbies,

A house of sparkplugs.

There is an entirely steel kitchen.

There is a self,

and a remainder of the self.

You don't have jowls.

You have immoral junk,

a cup of brain pox.

We feel tricked,

like always growing up beside a fern.

I feel like a compass at this little table.
Rheumy from sleep,
radiating from both ends.
What's settled now
will not always be settled.
I think we know this.
See: foxtrot, sarcophagus;
see: sacred.

See this shadow of the radiator,

closed eyes over a stairway.

See me woolen on the linoleum.

Blonde hair shaping

what is glass.

Strung up in heirlooms,
you jut out into the fog.
The owner of many hands
all of which I am familiar with.

The paint over our doorway is still wet.
We find and arrange coffee grounds
on the granite counters.
We hose down the flowers
and never see a flood.

Light breaks on the crown of your head.
Untroubled, you sit on the gray carpet.
A cricket keeps me awake.

Our body parts are alive,
full of living things,
as one might say
a terrarium is alive.

We hear whispers from the floor above.
The bathroom tiles sweat
and the ceiling drips
so we fall asleep in the park.

There is a room in here,
and inside of the room
there is a book about volcanoes.
In the book a little girl's arms are burning
to create speaking.

You have memorized the room,
its museum sound,
what the little girl meant.

What if we never find a place to live?
What is your favorite trimester?

In the kitchen we open the door to science.
The end of the year
is always coming up on us.

This is exquisite, this open concept.
Elsewhere a load-bearing wall,
a dangerous business.
We have no use for parquet floors,
for predictable rooms,
for pure function.

We still love those we hear
on the porch downstairs,
still walk all night in the bare mulch.

We leave the radio on to drown out
the sound of water leaking.

I have stopped thinking
that children are everywhere.

You are so glad in the dark of the porch
asking me to cook for you,
the ovens a short distance away,
heating and heating.

Don't you love the ocean?
Sometimes I hear all of it in separate rooms.
Rooms that spot us squarely.
Rooms full of water towers.
In our house, pockets are nervous
and for thirty-odd years
open out onto the floor.

Give me those arms.
It looks like we've covered
a lot of ground here, tall versions
of selves in the French cinema.
The acoustics unbelievable.

We needn't ever count nickels again
or unpack the bedclothes,
although I would be
straw in our house.
I would hold our children to the sky.

Anything the ocean,

Anything dance halls and ballets.

How social pale morning was.

I wonder if I'll ever see you alone again.

Outside, your coconut is leaking out onto the lawn.

Only the restlessness in a kitchen,

overage, as if

siphoning off hours

under the stove,

coils in apertures,

or mice,

or milk.

Welcome, cipher.

Welcome, recession.

Welcome each other.

Summer loves us too,

builds us up

to lumber, wooden.

Hoping for something curious,

as in, the road is to Providence.

Just get on and get going.

Acknowledgments

Many thanks to the editors of the following publications in which some of these poems first appear, sometimes in slightly earlier forms: *Bateau, Better: Culture and Lit, Coconut, Columbia: A Journal of Literature and Art, Denver Quarterly, For Penelope* (Factory Hollow Press), *Glitterpony, H_NGM_N, inDigest, interrupture, Los Angeles Review, Microfilme, The New Megaphone, Octopus, Parcel, Route 9, Sixth Finch, Souvenir, Spoke Too Soon: A Journal of the Longer,* and *Volt.*

"Poem to John Wayne" is for Mamama and Granddaddy.
"Hinge" is grateful to *Joseph Cornell's Theater of the Mind.*
"Earth Movements" is for Anne Cecelia Holmes.
"Containers" is for Caroline Cabrera.
"Poem to John Denver" is for Jessica Dylan Miele.
"Coward Order" is grateful to Sunderland, Massachusetts.

So much love and gratitude to my immense family—especially Mom, Dad, Lane, and Ryan—who have encouraged and supported me throughout the years.

Thank you to Carol Ann Davis, whose guidance helped me to learn the process for myself. Endless eternal thanks to Dara Wier, Peter Gizzi, James Haug, James Tate, and the community of writers at the University of Massachusetts–Amherst MFA Program for Poets and Writers, for their brilliance and support.

Thank you to my comrades, Anne Cecelia Holmes and Caroline Cabrera. A three in the morning thank you to Jessica Dylan Miele. Thank you to my brilliant friends and allies: Kelin Loe, Mike Wall, David Bartone, Ben Kopel, Matt Suss, Brian Foley, Mike Young, Philip Muller, Matthew Gifford, Kate Litterer, and Rachael Katz. Thank you, Jenny Krichevsky and Lauren Silber, for the Cherry Street love and kitchen.

Thank you to my new Georgia division: B. J. Love, Erika Jo Brown, Andrew Zawacki, Ed Pavlic, Dan Rosenberg, John Brown Spiers, Alex Edwards, Gina Abelkop, Paul Rodgers, Marni Ludwig, E. G. Cunningham, and my TVUS ladies—Alicia Rebecca Myers, Magdalena Zurawski, Jenny Gropp, and Laura Solomon.

Infinite gratitude goes to Nate Pritts for his constant generosity and encouragement, and to Tupelo Press—to Jeffrey Levine, Jim Schley, Bill Kuch, and Marie Gauthier—for taking in this little book, and for supporting what we do so lovingly.

Finally, I cannot imagine having written this book without Mamama and Grand-daddy's kitchen in Ridgeway, South Carolina. As Bachelard says, "through poems, perhaps more than through recollections, we touch the ultimate poetic depth of the space of the house." And I agree with him 100%.

Other Books from Tupelo Press

See our complete backlist at www.tupelopress.org

CPSIA information can be obtained
at www.ICGtesting.com
Printed in the USA
FFOW03n2258081214